Paul Newman

A Biography of the Legendary Actor

Andrew Cooper

Table of Contents

Introduction 1

Childhood In Shaker Heights, Ohio 3

World War II 5

After The War, A Focus On Theater 6

New York Theater Calls 8

The Silver Chalice (1954) 11

Rocky Graziano 13

The Long Hot Summer (1958) With Joanne 15

Moving Away From Typecasting 18

Rebels Without A Cause? 21

Paul Newman: Political Activist 24

Butch And Sundance 26

Newman's Introduction To Racing 28

First Artists 31

The Sting (1973) 33

The Towering Inferno (1974) 36

Working With Robert Altman 37

The Life And Death Of Scott Newman 39

Champion Race Car Driver 41

Newman's Own 44

Newman In The 1980s 45

The Return Of Fast Eddie Felson 48

Newman The Actor And Newman The Director 50

The Transformation Of Paul Newman's Racing Career 53

The Hole In The Wall Gang Camp 55

Newman's Films In The 1990s And Beyond 58

Cars (2006) 60

Newman's Own Foundation's Continuing Work 61

Charity Beyond Newman's Own Foundation 63

Philanthropic Awards 65

One Last Lap 67

Conclusion 69

Introduction

For well over 50 years Paul Newman was a cultural icon, a movie star and film director, a champion race car driver who earned his place among other professional racers, a famously devoted husband, a lauded philanthropist, and fairly consistently considered one of the best-looking men in the world. So much fuss was made about his piercing blue eyes that he once joked he would die a failure if his eyes should ever turn brown.

Coming into the Hollywood spotlight with the likes of Marlon Brando and James Dean in a new era of film stardom, Newman was a different breed of performer, one of the new method actors. Newman preferred to take on challenging and unusual parts that would test the limits of his abilities rather than opt for easy "leading-man" roles that only capitalized on his good looks and charm. Many of his movies are now considered classics.

In an industry where marriages seldom survive, he was married to actress Joanne Woodward for 50 years. What's more, his charitable foundation, based on the profits from his line of "Newman's Own" products, continues to donate millions of dollars each year to Newman's SeriousFun organization, which focuses on summer camps and outreach programs for sick children and their families.

But Paul Newman was not easy to know. He shied away from the paparazzi and photographers and was seldom happy to be interviewed, even limiting his appearances to promote his own films. He didn't like the press and wasn't comfortable speaking with them, and he certainly didn't like photographers either. Though the Hollywood gossip machine was frequently prone to spread rumors about troubles in his marriage to Joanne (periodically, they would be accused of being on the verge of divorce) the couple maintains that this was never true. There even came a point when they took out a prank ad promising to get a divorce to satisfy the reporters even though they "still liked each other."

Newman kept his private life very private indeed, living his family life in a small Connecticut town rather than in Hollywood. Being a sex symbol or a superstar meant nothing to him except as a way to influence matters that were important to him, including politics and charity. He was always a very serious, practiced and methodical performer, yet he admitted at times that audiences seemed to misunderstand his intentions, seeing him as an anti-hero when he felt he was clearly playing a villain. It seemed that no matter how bad a character he played audiences continued to love watching him.

Friends and family members talk about a different side of Newman, however. He was, they say, hilarious, an elaborate prankster and joker (especially to his close friends, such as Robert Redford), and always ready to have some fun. In the midst of serious preparation - his wife of 50 years, Joanne Woodward, says that Newman prepared thoroughly for everything he did - he was kind, charming, funny and always a joy to be around. His friends call him grounded, generous, funny, professional, and the women seemed to find him the ideal of masculine appeal. Newman was eager and enthusiastic about life.

Childhood in
Shaker Heights, Ohio

P aul Leonard Newman was born on January 26, 1925, to parents Arthur and Theresa Newman. He was the Newmans' second son; his older brother was Arthur Jr., and the pair of them stuck together closely throughout childhood, each always ready to defend the other. Paul's father was Jewish and his mother a Christian Science believer; Paul would usually identify as Jewish throughout his life although he really practiced no religion. The Newmans lived in the affluent Shaker Heights suburb of Cleveland, Ohio, and here Paul was raised. His father was a partner/owner in a successful sporting goods store in Cleveland called Newman Stern.

Paul considered his father Arthur both brilliant and emotionally distant. In his own life experience, Newman seemed to reflect that behavior, wishing in later years that he had been more emotionally available to his own children. Newman's mother, Theresa, was passionate about theater, and at the time, Cleveland was a great place to find theatrical outlets. Theresa encouraged her son to try out for plays. At 8 years of age, he played a court jester in a production of *Robin Hood*. He even sang a song that had been written by his Uncle Joe (also a theater fan).

Cleveland's community theater has, since the turn of the 20th century, had a proud and important historic significance in the area (just for example, it was the location of Margaret Hamilton's stage debut in the 1920s, before she went to Hollywood to gain fame as the Wicked Witch of the West). The theater remained enormously influential in Cleveland during Paul's childhood. Paul was a member of the Cleveland Playhouse's children's theater program, established in 1933 and believed to be the first free theatrical education program for children. The group was later renamed the "Curtain Pullers," and Paul is certainly one member of whom they like to boast. Another renowned actor who had his debut through the Curtain Pullers was Joel Grey. Through their organization, at age 10, Paul was in a production of *Saint George and the Dragon.*

Though Paul grew up handsome (and was complimented quite early and often for his piercing blue eyes), his childhood friends say he was either unaware or unconcerned about his good looks, more interested in games and sports, always funny and never terribly serious.

After high school, Paul became a fairly successful encyclopedia salesman, and Paul used encyclopedia sales to make ends meet and support his family throughout his early acting career both before and after World War II. His natural charm made him a good salesman (in fact, he was so good at it that he was able to sell his route later for about $500, according to one of his old friends who didn't do quite as well). It is easy - and amusing - to imagine the many housewives who answered their doors to be sold encyclopedias by this handsome young man. Cleveland had probably never seen such an interest in learning.

World War II

In 1943, Paul enlisted in the Naval Air Corps and was sent to Yale for officers' training. He wanted to be a pilot but it was discovered that he was color blind, making him ineligible. Paul enlisted instead as a radio operator and rear gunner for naval planes in the Pacific theater (Hawaii, Guam and Okinawa). An earache suffered by his airplane's pilot, which resulted in the entire crew being grounded, was the only reason Paul was not aboard the *Bunker Hill* aircraft carrier when it was attacked by a kamikaze flyer, causing the deaths of a number of troops. Both Paul and Arthur Newman Jr. were able to return home after the war.

After the War,
a Focus on Theater

At 21, Newman returned to Shaker Heights and enrolled in Ohio's Kenyon College. There, he studied literature and drama and was a linebacker on the football team. But after a game one night, he was arrested for fighting in a local bar. This was when he was thrown off the football team and was "forced" to devote all his time to acting, such as performing the male lead in the college's production of *The Front Page*.

Paul graduated in 1949 with a Bachelor of Science degree. He was actually expected to return to Shaker Heights to work in the family business. Paul, however, had the acting bug and wanted to make a career out of it. Within two hours of his graduation, Paul was on the train to Williams Bay, Wisconsin, to spend a season in summer stock. After that, he joined the Woodstock Players in Woodstock, Illinois, a sort of "proving ground" of intense theater productions that put on a new show every week but also required the actors to build the sets. Here, he met fellow actor Tom Bosley, who recalls that Newman was fond of goofing off between building sets, a fun guy who loved beer and popcorn. He was nevertheless a serious dramatic student.

Newman also met and began a relationship with 19-year-old actress Jackie Witte, who was also doing summer theater work. Their romance was fiery and quick, and they were married quite soon after they began dating. They would remain married from 1949 to 1958 and would have three children: Scott, Susan and Stefanie. For much of this time Jackie had to get by on her own as Paul pursued acting jobs, but Jackie was also able to visit New York and work as a model. Newman later contemplated that he and Jackie were too young and inexperienced and got married too quickly to realize that they were not a good lifetime match.

However, for a time around the birth of their first child, it seemed Paul Newman might give up acting entirely to become a businessman as his own father had intended. Arthur Newman Sr. became seriously ill in 1949, and Paul returned to Shaker Heights to help his family. His father died in 1950 without ever having seen Paul act professionally, and perhaps it always bothered Paul that his father had never seen him succeed at anything. It was expected that Paul Newman should take over the family's sporting goods business at the time, but Newman could not bring himself to do so; Paul Newman was seldom a man who could do anything for which he had no passion, and he certainly had no passion for merchandising. Not yet, anyway; that would come later when it seemed the profits could be used to help others.

Paul's son Scott was born shortly after Arthur Newman Sr.'s death. This prompted Paul to make a serious effort at a stable career in theater, but he only intended to teach college theatrical directing. Paul made the decision to sell his family's Cleveland business. Then, with the money from that sale, he enrolled at Yale as a graduate student to major in directing. Jackie stayed home with their baby while Paul worked and went to school. Paul's plan was to return to Kenyon College and teach directing. His desire to become a professional actor took second place to a more certain career path that could hopefully provide for his family.

New York Theater Calls

Paul Newman's career seems to be peppered with times when he was discovered almost by accident, days when he accompanied someone else and just happened to be in the right room in time to catch the eye of a teacher or a director. He might not have considered his physical appearance often, nor did he want to be known as a sex symbol, but clearly the handsome, charming, blue-eyed actor was an object of attention everywhere he went.

After only six months at Yale, during a performance, he was spotted by a husband/wife agent team who invited him to come to Manhattan to become a professional actor. He, Jackie and their children moved to Staten Island. He began receiving television roles fairly quickly.

There was a "new wave" of theater going on then. Tennessee Williams and Arthur Miller were revitalizing American theater with a new, gritty style of playwriting, and here also the Actor's Studio was teaching method acting, a fairly new concept, which was touted by the likes of Marlon Brando and James Dean.

Newman was very interested in joining the Actor's Studio but couldn't get an audition and confessed much later (to the Actor's Studio audience, in fact) that he got in by "sleight of hand." He agreed to help a friend with her second audition when her partner was called away on a job, so together they performed a scene from *Battle of Angels.* On the merit of that scene, Newman was invited to join the Studio. Newman jokes he was terrified during the performance and that they mistook his terror for anger.

Meanwhile, Newman was cast in the Broadway Play *Picnic* almost by accident, as he had gone to the William Morris agency with a friend and had been "spotted" in the waiting room by the show's director. He was put into the show as an understudy and due to the play's fourteen-month run had many opportunities to play parts when other actors were out.

Picnic was a big success that stayed in production for over a year. Working on the show, Newman met Joanne Woodward, another understudy, described as a "beautiful Southern belle" with a biting wit. Woodward, a former beauty queen who had studied drama in college, was several years younger than Newman. The first time she saw him it was an incredibly hot day, and she went into the agent's office just because it was air-conditioned. And there was Paul, she recalled, looking so cool and collected in his seersucker suit that she thought it was disgusting. (In response to this, Newman argues that it was his only suit, and he had to wash it every night!)

Though he and Joanne noticed each other, she was initially dismissive of him as just a pretty boy, and his shyness and reserve made her think he was dull. Eventually, during the show, they did form a friendship, and they remained in contact after the show was over. However, Paul was married and had a family at the time, and he was actually serious about his married life.

Thanks to the long run of *Picnic,* Newman was left without any financial worries or pressures to audition, and he was able to continue studying at the Actors' Studio.

While it is true that "method acting" was the new catchphrase for up-and-coming actors like Brando and Dean, Newman himself described "method acting" by saying the "method" was actually different for every actor, and that no actor was taught in the same way. Newman believed that he was helped a great deal by the Actor's Studio, where he was instructed by Geraldine Page and other highly respected actors and learned how to become more subtle and thoughtful in his approach to acting. Newman learned that acting is a process that should go so deeply that you should be able to see a character's thoughts turning over in the actor's eyes. Newman felt that the Studio was the most important factor in his ability to have an acting career. He says that the Actor's Studio must take either the "credit or the blame" for his skills. He likens an actor to a musical instrument and claims that the Actor's Studio experts develop and tune the instrument of each actor so that his or her skill is available to that actor when it is needed.

While in New York, Newman also received several small television parts from 1949 through 1954.

His performance in the long-running play *Picnic* got Newman attention in Hollywood. Talent scouts saw him as the next Marlon Brando. Newman was given a studio contract at $1,000 a week and screen-tested with James Dean for *East of Eden.* Obviously, Dean was cast in *East of Eden,* whereas Paul was cast in the 1954 film *The Silver Chalice,* a fictional story of a Greek slave who designed the chalice meant to hold the Holy Grail, made at a time when big biblical epics were box office gold in Hollywood.

The Silver Chalice (1954)

Paul Newman is certainly not the only actor to ever be embarrassed by his first starring role in a film, but he was particularly disgusted with this pseudo-biblical historical melodrama. Newman himself said it was probably "the worst film made during the entire decade of the '50s." As the Greek sculptor "Basil," he was embarrassed by his wooden performance and his silly costume (a short toga, which he claims he didn't "have the legs for"). Newman hated wearing a tunic so much that rumor has it, years later when he was considered for the titular role of *Ben-Hur*, he turned it down.

The film's critical reception for the most part was not precisely damning, with the worst complaints being that it was overly long and tedious, without including any interesting characters. In the following years, however, critics grew less kind, and *The Silver Chalice* gained a reputation for being truly bad, vulgar and boring, this opinion supported by Paul Newman's own dislike of the movie. Sometimes the film is referred to as *Paul Newman and the Holy Grail*.

To mitigate what he saw as *The Silver Chalice's* potentially serious damage to his acting career, Newman quickly put himself back on the stage in New York in a tense production of *The Desperate Hours*, and he also starred on television in a production of *Our Town*.

Many years later, when *The Silver Chalice* was set to premiere on television in 1966, Newman took out a full-page ad in the *Los Angeles Times* to apologize for his performance prior to the film's airing. Unfortunately, the ad backfired, generating great interest in the movie and resulting in record-high ratings for the film's on-air premiere.

Rocky Graziano

When he returned to film, things got better for Newman. In 1955, he was given the lead role in *Somebody Up There Likes Me* (which would premiere in 1956). As had been the case with *East of Eden,* he was up against James Dean again for the role. If Dean hadn't been tragically killed in a car accident, Paul might not have been cast.

The film was about boxing star Rocky Graziano; so, Paul studied the character seriously (including hanging out with Rocky Graziano himself and learned his mannerisms) and also took up a rigorous boxing regime. Newman practically lived with Graziano for a couple of weeks to study him, though he found that Graziano was more interested in hearing about Newman's life than in talking about his own.

Newman learned from Graziano that Marlon Brando also had studied Graziano for a certain amount of time, though more subtly than Newman had. Graziano had simply noticed this kid watching him work out for several weeks until finally the young man approached him and invited him to come see a play he was in, *A Streetcar Named Desire.* This is interesting because Newman was frequently compared to Brando in his early days (not always flatteringly, but as if Newman was no more than a Brando wannabe) and also frequently mistaken for Brando on the street. Newman estimates he might have signed up to 500 or so autographs as "Marlon Brando."

Somebody Up There Likes Me was well-received by critics, though one criticism was that Newman was not convincing as an Italian-American. Nevertheless, the film gave him another chance at being a respected actor. To this day the movie remains popular; it is now considered a classic sports movie, often referenced in best-of-sports-movies lists.

The Long
Hot Summer (1958) with Joanne

Martin Ritt, who had suffered from the blacklisting in Hollywood, returned to the spotlight when he directed *The Long Hot Summer*, which starred Orson Welles, Angela Lansbury, Paul Newman and Joanne Woodward. The film was both a critical and box-office success.

Newman made many strong connections in this film; first, he found himself highly compatible with director Ritt. He would work with Ritt again on many of his most famous movies (so, too, would Joanne Woodward, sometimes the pair of them together but more often, separately working with the director). Newman remembers Ritt as a "musical, physical" kind of director, and together they formed a shorthand of communication. Newman says that Ritt could convey in a sound or a gesture what he wanted from a scene, and it always made perfect sense.

Working with Orson Welles was also a pleasure if a rather mixed one. Welles was only too aware of his own genius and fame and was notoriously difficult on film sets. Nevertheless, the cast seems to recall Welles with great affection, calling him crafty, wonderful, diabolical, enigmatic - and Newman accuses him basically of being a scene-stealer. No matter what the scene or who it featured, if Welles was in it, it was Welles' scene. He recalls being in awe of the man and of Welles teasing the Actor's Studio alumni for their mumbling and "method acting."

Of course, the most life-changing meeting Newman had during the filming was his reunion with actress Joanne Woodward. Woodward had won the Best Actress Oscar the year before for her performance in *The Three Faces of Eve*, so she too was a particularly hot commodity in the film business at the time. The pair played a romantic couple with high sexual tension in the film, and this certainly reflected real life. Though he was still married to Jackie Witte at the time, he separated from her and began a "quiet" affair with Joanne. Her description of the affair was a good deal racier, mentioning that their on-screen chemistry led to many an "interesting" meeting in motel rooms. Jackie Witte reluctantly granted Paul a divorce when it became clear that he would not be returning to her.

The wrap-up of filming on *The Long Hot Summer* coincided with the granting of Newman's divorce, and within a month, Newman and Woodward ran away to El Rancho Vegas to have a quick wedding ceremony. They then went for a honeymoon in London.

In a later biographical interview, Newman admitted that he always carried the guilt of breaking up his first marriage the way he did and perhaps wishes he had handled the situation better or differently. Nevertheless, he and Joanne Woodward went on to break all the Hollywood stereotypes for marriages by remaining married for 50 years in an industry where marriages far more typically end in divorce and acrimony.

Newman and Joanne Woodward moved to Westport, Connecticut, (another unusual practice for Hollywood stars at the time) where they bought an 18th-century farmhouse on 15 acres. Together, he and Joanne had three daughters, Elinor (1959), Melissa (1961) and Claire (1965). Despite his growing worldwide fame, Newman stayed grounded with his wife and family, always feeling most comfortable when he was connected with them.

Over the years to come, Newman and Woodward would appear in ten films together and the HBO miniseries, *Empire Falls*. Newman also directed four films in which Woodward starred, and the pair of them returned in various incarnations to the theater to work together, such as starring in the run of the play *Baby Want a Kiss* in 1964.

Moving
Away from Typecasting

In 1959, Newman appeared in *Cat on a Hot Tin Roof* and received his first Oscar nomination for Best Actor. At that point, he bought out his contract with Warner Brothers for $500,000, to become a free agent so he could take more challenging roles. He was worried about getting typecast in Hollywood and being packaged as a piece of "beefcake." He did not want to constantly be in "leading man" roles.

The flaw in his logic was that, as he was widely considered one of the most handsome men in film and had a screen presence and magnetism that was hard to deny, he became the "leading man" in most of his films, regardless of his intentions. This is not to say that he wasn't choosing challenging and unusual parts; only that in playing these parts, he created a string of unforgettable anti-heroes that fit in perfectly with an era of civil and youthful unrest.

He quickly made several notable films, including *From the Terrace* (again with Joanne Woodward), a movie in which he played a part quite similar to his own life story. His character was a young man expected to follow in his father's footsteps in business but ultimately lacking the values or skills that his father demanded of him. Newman was only too aware of the pain of disappointing a father figure.

Exodus was a project of some personal interest to him because of his Jewish roots. His co-star, Eve Marie Saint, found Newman to be quite level-headed, a serious performer yet a man with a lighthearted attitude.

It was in 1961 that Newman caught real critical and social attention with his part of "Fast Eddie" Felson in *The Hustler,* a movie made famous by its sheer, gritty style and Newman's irredeemable con artist. There had been few films made like this before, and it certainly set the stage for a new breed of angst-ridden, discontented storytelling. Newman received his second Oscar nomination for this part. The movie is now considered an American classic, and Newman's performance marked as one of the most memorable in his career. He would reprise the role again in 1986 for the film *The Color of Money* - more on that later!

In 1962, Newman reprised his stage role in the film *Sweet Bird of Youth,* directed by Elia Kazan. When Newman is interviewed about his career, he seldom relays the story of any person without saying what he learned from that individual, for Newman was always studying and improving himself. He found working with Kazan to be extremely educational, saying that Kazan was an expert in keeping him both happy and unbalanced at the same time and that Kazan taught him about changing up the rhythm of dialog and letting his character think ahead.

Kazan gave Newman pointers on pacing sentences and scenes without the ordinary beats, and as Newman recalls, "If you want to make a point with a pause, you can't pause all the time. You can't make a point by yelling if you're yelling all the time." The trick, however, was that Kazan showed him these things without destroying his self-confidence. Newman used this technique later when he directed films. He feels that a director's job is to give actors the confidence and the tools they need to really reach for something special; it takes something different for each actor.

It is always interesting to listen as Newman describes himself and his method of acting in terms of a musical instrument that is meant to be played. He believed in "honing his instrument" - that is, as an actor, he was the instrument through which a part could be played and that instrument should always be tuned in such a way that he can summon his skills at a moment's notice. When, as an older actor, he looked back on his early roles, he would criticize his technique: he was too big, trying too hard, and scratching away at his instrument - it seems he was always his own worst critic. In later years, he found it difficult to watch his early films because to him, he seemed to be so "out of tune."

Rebels Without a Cause?

If James Dean and Marlon Brando were known for creating the archetype of the dissatisfied and rebellious youth of the 1950s and '60s, then Paul Newman was known for taking that youth and making him likable. Famed film critic Pauline Kael once said that no one should be asked not to like Paul Newman; he simply projected frankness and sweetness to the point that the audience felt compelled to protect him from all harm.

In 1963, Newman starred as the title character of Hud Bannon in the classic American neo-western film *Hud.* The film was directed by Newman's friend Martin Ritt, with whom he had a deeply compatible director-to-actor relationship. The character of Hud is an irredeemably heartless man whose immoral behavior has a negative effect on everyone around him. He's technically meant to be the villain of the piece.

Newman and Ritt wanted Hud, the character, to be like a modern-day Iago, and the audience caught every nuance of this villainy *except* for the corruption. For all the work that Ritt and Newman did to make it clear that Hud was a bad man, the character captured the imagination of the anti-establishment, anti-hero-loving crowd of moviegoers at the time. Apparently, a combination of civil unrest plus Paul Newman's natural good looks and charm made it impossible to see the morally bankrupt Hud for what he really was; instead, he just became "misunderstood."

In 1966, Newman got to star in Alfred Hitchcock's spy thriller, *Torn Curtain*; unfortunately, the movie was critically panned as being both poorly cast and boring. Newman was in a few other films as well that were not terribly well-known or popular at the box office. He really returned to form in 1967, when he made two films that reinvigorated his image as the iconic anti-hero.

The first was *Hombre*, once more made with his friend Martin Ritt directing. In this film, Newman is a white man who was raised by Apache Indians, and although he is clearly blue-eyed and blond, he still must endure the racism of other white people against the family and people who raised him. The film was an interesting view of racism in that it did not preach its lessons but let the audience simply sit back and watch, drawing our own conclusions. Newman's character must make a decision late in the film as to whether he will protect the very people who have shunned him socially.

But by far the most career-defining role Newman took in 1967 was that of Luke in the classic chain-gang drama *Cool Hand Luke*, a movie that has stood the test of time to become a beloved cinematic standard. It's a fascinating film to watch, as it mostly consists of Paul Newman's character Lucas "Luke" Jackson subjecting himself to needless torment just because of his stubborn refusal to conform to rules; he seems to delight in irritating the authority figures who have control over his life and uses his rebellion as a way to gain respect and friendship among his desperate fellow inmates. Yet somehow, as usual, Newman's charm makes it all more than palatable. Despite the near futility of the character's actions, *Cool Hand Luke* is nevertheless ceaselessly entertaining. Newman works with an incredibly strong supporting cast. It is now one of the "Great Movies" as listed by Roger Ebert and appears in the book *1001 Movies You Must See Before You Die.*

Paul Newman: Political Activist

Newman was a Democrat for life, and what's more, a Democrat of such prominent social standing that he was eventually placed nineteenth on Richard Nixon's "enemies list" (a real list made by then-President Nixon, which has now become something of a cultural in-joke). Also, it should be noted that being on President Nixon's enemies list was a matter of considerable pride for the actor; he called it "one of his greatest achievements."

Newman's inclusion on the infamous list was due to the actor's vocal opposition to the Vietnam War and his support of Eugene McCarthy in the 1968 election. McCarthy's campaign platform was based heavily on influencing the government to decrease, if not stop, U.S. military activity in Vietnam. McCarthy was an extremely popular figure among anti-war protestors. However, McCarthy eventually lost the nomination to Vice President Hubert Humphrey, and those who had followed McCarthy turned their support to Humphrey in hopes that if Humphrey were victorious, he would also take on the job of extricating the U.S. from Vietnam. During the general election of 1968, Newman also transferred his support to Hubert Humphrey and appeared on a pre-election night telethon in support of the politician.

Newman's political leanings were never quite as vocal as they were in 1968, but he did continue to support democratic causes and candidates. Other politicians for whom Newman showed support were:

- ⅄ **Ned Lamont**: Newman supported Lamont in the 2006 Connecticut Democratic Primary against Senator Joe Lieberman, based on the fact that Lieberman showed a conciliatory and supportive relationship with Republican leadership.

- ⅄ **Chris Dodd**: Newman contributed money to Dodd's campaign for Democratic nomination for presidency, which was focused in opposition to the Iraq War.

- ⅄ **Bill Richardson:** Newman also contributed money to Richardson's campaign for election. Richardson has acted as U.S. Ambassador to the United Nations and is a well-known diplomatic troubleshooter.

Newman worked in support of many liberal causes. He attended the March on Washington in 1963. He was present for the festivities on the first Earth Day event in April 1970. From an early time, Newman was a vocal supporter of same-sex marriage and gay rights. He also supported nuclear energy development as a clean-energy alternative to help prevent global warming.

Newman also supported and participated in the publication of *The Nation*, a long-running, left-wing weekly periodical. In 1995, he joined with a group to purchase the magazine and support it financially; it was not a publication that made steady income. Rumor has it the magazine only made a profit four times during its continuing publication, which is now approaching 150 years. Over the years, Newman also contributed several wryly-written articles to the weekly journal.

Butch and Sundance

In speaking about the film *Butch Cassidy and the Sundance Kid* (1969), many years later on *Inside the Actor's Studio,* Newman claimed that it was hard for him now to separate fact from fiction. The movie has become so culturally iconic that it has replaced the real history of the gunfighters as well as some of the history of Newman and Robert Redford with a series of tall tales about their friendship. The movie tells the story of two train robbers who become notorious enough that they are pursued by a "super posse" that drives them to escape to Bolivia. The majority of the film concerns their long flight from pursuit.

The film was originally titled *The Sundance Kid and Butch Cassidy* and was meant to star Steve McQueen as the Sundance Kid. When McQueen dropped out, Paul Newman was the biggest star and so the title was switched to having his character's name first. As a replacement for McQueen, Warren Beatty was considered, but he declined, thinking the film was too much like *Bonnie and Clyde.* Newman, however, had noticed and been impressed by younger actor Robert Redford, and director George Roy Hill agreed with him. The studio was not eager to hire Redford, who was not yet well-known, but Newman and Hill kept insisting until it was agreed to bring the actor in.

Newman and Redford (who was habitually late to set, Newman often noted) became lifelong friends during the filming, and their personal chemistry and camaraderie were so obvious that it transferred easily onto film, adding to its aura of a great "buddy movie" and sometimes called a platonic love story between two men. The two actors were both very alike, politically motivated, with strong family ties. Both hated being sex symbols and were shy and impatient with attention from fans and media. Redford says that working on *Butch and Sundance* was the most fun he ever had on a film.

The movie, once released, was critic-proof; despite mediocre and even mocking reviews, word of mouth got around about the film's fun and humor, the film crushed the box office several weeks in a row. Yet again, Newman was in a role that showed "contempt for authority" and an anti-hero being dogged constantly by "the system" (the posse that chases the two lead characters being an easy stand-in for the government).

The movie remains as popular as ever today, a beloved American classic thanks, in large part, to the chemistry between the actors. Adjusted for inflation, it is the highest-grossing western film ever made; by today's numbers, it has grossed over half a billion dollars. In 2007, the film was ranked by the American Film Institute as number 73 in its list of the Greatest Movies of All Time; and the characters of Butch and Sundance are co-ranked at number 20 on AFI's list of greatest screen heroes (a point of interest: on this same list, Luke Jackson from *Cool Hand Luke* appears at number 30).

Newman's
Introduction to Racing

Newman's older brother, Arthur Newman Jr., recollects that he and Paul had no access to cars when they were growing up in Shaker Heights. Their father did not see automobiles as a necessity for young people, and even after both Arthur and Paul had returned from serving in World War II and were starting college, neither of them had a car.

In 1967, Newman approached race car driver Mario Andretti. When they met, Andretti asked Newman if he would like to take a ride in the car. Newman naturally agreed and held on with white knuckles as Andretti took him around the track. Andretti believes this was where Paul became hooked on the idea of driving.

Newman starred in two films released in 1969: *Butch Cassidy and the Sundance Kid* and *Winning*. Both films played a part in introducing Newman to what many call his greatest passion: automobile racing. The connection between *Winning* and his new career was more obvious: for the role, Newman and co-star Robert Wagner both had to take race car driving lessons at the famous Bob Bondurant School of Driving. Robert Wagner recalls attending the driving lessons and being "relieved" when the intense driving sessions were over but remembers that Newman would continue to speed around the track as long as they would let him. Newman practiced with Indy cars and the Ford GT40 and did so well with the driving that he insisted on doing his own stunt driving for the film. In fact, on the Internet Movie Database it is his only credit for stunt work.

Meanwhile, on the set of *Butch and Sundance*, Newman was becoming fast friends with Robert Redford, a young actor for whom Newman served as an inspiration and mentor. They had a great deal in common, and one such shared interest was cars. Redford had a collection of race cars himself and asked Newman if he would like to drive Redford's Porsche 904. Newman did so and clearly loved it.

Paul's connections in the movie world were not eager for him to turn to race car driving. He was far too valuable of a film commodity for them to be comfortable with the risks involved. Joanne Woodward shared in their concerns, more for the sake of his safety than his box office value, of course, but it seemed nothing would sway Newman from his desire to race professionally. He said in later interviews about his seduction to the racing circuit that he had always wanted to be a sportsman but had no personal grace. He was bad at football, bad at running, and bad at pool, and the only place he ever found grace was behind the wheel of a car.

But Paul was nothing if not methodical and purposeful in everything he tried. As his wife Joanne said, he prepared for everything he did. Newman was a strong believer in practice and allowing for mistakes. Mistakes, he figured, were the way one learned. He began to practice driving with the Bob Sharp Datsun team. Expert driver Bob Sharp told Newman that if he really wanted to learn how to race cars, he needed to drive for a couple of years in an underpowered car so he could focus on learning technique rather than on trying to win.

At the Lime Rock Raceway in Lakeville, Connecticut, Paul took lessons from driver Sam Posey, who became a close personal friend. (An interesting tidbit: Sam Posey's wife, an artist, would later design the "Newman's Own" product labels.) Sam Posey recalls that at first, Newman was a "terrible" driver. Yet Newman continued to diligently work in his little, underpowered Datsun 510 on practice days, telling Posey that he was learning to play the part of a race car driver. His willingness to learn from his mistakes and take advice gained respect for him among the racing staff at Lime Rock.

Robert Redford eventually went to visit Lime Rock to see how Newman was coming along. Redford drove the track himself, then watched Newman drive it in half the time and realized how good his friend was getting. Redford jokingly says that from that point on, Newman got boring: all he wanted to talk about was cars.

First Artists

In 1969, Newman formed a film production company with Sidney Poitier and Barbra Streisand, "First Artists." The idea for the small film company was that of the Creative Management agency, and the business plan was inspired by United Artists, the production company famously formed in 1919 by Mary Pickford and Douglas Fairbanks, among others, specifically to give actors more control over their interests rather than forcing them to rely on studios. The purpose of the First Artists company was, like United Artists, to give acting talent more freedom to choose their projects and exercise creative control. The three actors agreed to make smaller, more "independent" films and take smaller paychecks (and a cut of the profits) in exchange for that creative control.

Newman, Streisand and Poitier each agreed to make three movies for First Artists. Steve McQueen joined the company soon after its formation, and Dustin Hoffman became a member in 1972. First Artists made some films that were fairly successful, such as *The Getaway* (1972) and *The Life and Times of Judge Roy Bean* (1972), but after almost six years in business, the company had only made seven films.

It seems no one problem alone can be blamed for the mediocre performance of First Artists, but several different issues were at play:

scheduling conflicts kept the stars from being freely available; their "creative control" over movies could only be allowed if the films were on schedule and under budget, something that many films under the creative control of inexperienced actor-management failed to do. In an effort to keep the company in the black, certain compromises had to be made for film distribution, which seemed to undermine the original concept of the organization – that of creative freedom.

A flurry of lawsuits erupted between First Artists and other parties (including both Steve McQueen and Dustin Hoffman) when it seemed that promises of "creative freedom" only lasted insofar as the films were made under budget, on time, and were ultimately successful. The company left the movie business in 1979 after having made just over 20 films (three of which were made for television).

In addition to *Roy Bean,* Paul Newman made *Pocket Money* (1972) and *The Drowning Pool* (1975) for First Artists, so three films in total, as he had agreed. Despite First Artists' later conflicts, Newman's experience with the company went according to plan and serves as another example of Newman's entrepreneurial spirit and his belief in doing unusual, challenging projects.

The Sting (1973)

For a few years after 1968, Newman continued to take on roles that presented him with learning opportunities, unique challenges and the thrill of playing against type, but his box office returns slumped. Aside from the comedy *The Life and Times of Judge Roy Bean* (1972), the films *WUSA, Sometimes a Great Notion, Pocket Money,* and *The Mackintosh Man* made little money and garnered little attention.

However, by 1973 he and Robert Redford had agreed to team up again with director George Roy Hill to make *The Sting*. In truth, the director was initially to be David S. Ward, the screenwriter, who had never directed before. Also, on first pass, both Redford and Newman declined roles in the film. Redford didn't trust Ward to direct, and Newman thought himself too young to play the role of Henry Gondorff. After the roles of Henry Gondorff and Johnny Hooker were offered and turned down or denied to a seemingly endless parade of then-popular actors (Jack Nicholson, Warren Beatty, Peter Boyle, Lee Van Cleef, and Robert Wagner) and Hill was replaced as the director of the movie, Redford and Newman agreed to work once more with their Butch & Sundance director, so the trio was together again.

From the time he read the script, Newman felt this was "first-class" material, and if everyone did their job, the film would turn out to be a winner.

The film was meant to completely evoke the time period of gangster and prohibition warfare in 1930s Chicago. George Roy Hill deliberately filmed the movie in the style of the 1930s (i.e., without using a lot of extras in scenes or using stylistic wipes to transition from one scene to another) to put the audience in the frame of mind for the 1930s. The ragtime music of Scott Joplin was heavily employed to evoke this mood but was an anachronistic error; ragtime was popular a good 20 years prior to the film's events. Nevertheless, Joplin's ragtime tunes are inextricably linked with the movie now.

Newman and Redford continued to play jokes on each other throughout the filming. Though crowds often gathered at their location scenes and they gathered a great deal of attention, neither actor let it get to them, instead concentrating on their parts. Newman is said to have taken the part of Harry Gondorff because he wanted to play a comic role; however, Hill typically instructed him to play his part seriously. Nevertheless, the chemistry of the starring duo remained one of the film's biggest draws, dressed up as it was in a beautifully made homage to 1930s gangster pics and the glamour of old Hollywood.

The year of its premiere, *The Sting* won the Best Picture Academy Award (along with six other Oscars). It has since been selected for preservation by the National Film Registry. It is considered a classic and, like a good number of Newman's other films as we've seen, often appears in Top 100 "best film" lists.

The film revitalized Newman's career.

The Sting was also the last picture that Neman and Redford did together, though they were always willing to do another if a good script had come along. Redford says they were offered sequels to both *Butch & Sundance* and *The Sting*, but neither wanted to do either film. They both wanted to wait for a great script – but unfortunately one never materialized. The two actors only performed together casually on stage after that (at charity fundraisers).

However, Newman does tell a funny story of being offered the part in a sequel to Redford's film *Indecent Proposal* (a 1993 film in which Redford's wealthy character pays a young couple a million dollars for the chance to sleep with the wife). The film did well enough at the box office that a sequel was contemplated. Newman was asked jokingly asked if he would "shack up" with Redford for a million dollars in *Indecent Proposal 2*. Newman replied yes, and that, in fact, he would shack up with a gorilla for a million dollars. "A male gorilla?" Newman was asked, in response to which Newman asked for an additional 10 percent. Then, Redford was contacted and given the same offer; "Newman will shack up with you for a million dollars in *Indecent Proposal 2*." Redford said, after a pause, that a million wasn't enough.

The Towering Inferno (1974)

T he very next year after appearing in *The Sting,* Newman co-starred in cult classic disaster film, *The Towering Inferno.* Newman got $1 million for the film. He did his own stunts for the action extravaganza.

Newman co-starred with Steve McQueen. The studio heads had some concerns that Newman and McQueen would not be able to work well on set together, as both of them were known for being similarly serious about their parts and reputedly quite competitive toward each other. Some stories that were bandied around were, for example, that McQueen insisted he and Newman have the same number of lines and the same amount of screen time. However, in person, Newman and Steve McQueen got along surprisingly well and had a great time together.

Of course, the film itself was an enormous box office hit, joining the ranks of *The Poseidon Adventure* and *Airport* as blockbuster disaster films of the 1970s. Also, during the filming of *Towering Inferno*, Newman got to work with his son Scott Newman on the picture, though they never had any dialog and only technically one scene together. At the time, Scott was struggling with serious issues of increasingly troubling alcoholism.

Working with Robert Altman

N ewman made two films with innovative director Robert Altman, neither of which is well-known in either man's repertoire. They worked together in 1976 on *Buffalo Bill and the Indians* and again in 1979 on *Quintet.* Newman remembers in both cases that he worked very hard on the characters, as was always his practice.

In *Buffalo Bill,* Altman and Newman tried to upend an American legend of heroism, with Newman playing the real-life Buffalo Bill who lived out his career performing in a Wild West show. Newman liked the idea of playing the character because he was, in Newman's opinion, a forerunner to the phenomenon of the movie star "celebrity" lifestyle. Critically, the movie was called pretentious, dull and overlong, and Altman was accused of wasting Newman's talents by giving him nothing much to do. The film did, however, receive some critical praise for being innovative.

Quintet was a post-apocalyptic tale that takes place while a new ice age ravages earth and the dying populace finds some entertainment in betting on human lives in the bizarre, titular survival game. *Quintet* found even less critical success than *Buffalo Bill,* with critics mostly puzzled or annoyed by its heavy-handed symbolism and easily bored with its depressing, confusing story. The movie hasn't aged well either and is seldom referenced when one is discussing Newman's career. That being said, the role was another challenging risk for the actor, who always went for the difficult parts rather than the easy "leading man" roles. To play a post-apocalyptic survivor in a frozen wasteland was certainly playing against type for Newman at the time.

The Life and
Death of Scott Newman

S cott Newman, the first child of Paul Newman and Jackie Witte, always
seemed to have one foot in trouble. He was 8 years old at the time his
parents divorced, and Paul Newman himself had admitted that he had
not been as emotionally available to his children as he should have been. Scott
attended a number of expensive private schools and was expelled from many
of them for bad behavior.

Scott dropped out of college in order to pursue a career as a stuntman. He
became a certified parachute jumping instructor and also worked other menial
jobs, refusing to take money from his father. Though he claimed he did not
want to accept any career help from his father, Scott was nevertheless a
stuntman on many of Paul Newman's films and was also secured a role in *The
Great Waldo Pepper* (1975), a Robert Redford movie, through Paul
Newman's influence.

Scott was a heavy drinker and often arrested for alcohol-related
offenses. Paul Newman confessed that he, too, had his own problems with
alcohol, and he seems to deeply regret this common ground he shared with
his son. Scott even assaulted a police officer while drunk, resulting in a fine
that had to be paid off, once more, by his father.

Scott had a role in *The Towering Inferno,* in which his father also starred, although he and Paul Newman had no dialog together and only shared one scene in the entire movie. Scott had the role of a firefighter. Scott also made a number of television appearances and was in Charles Bronson's film *Breakheart Pass* and in *Fraternity Row,* his last film appearance.

Scott had a deep, unhappy envy of his father's success, confessing to family friend A.E. Hotchner that he lacked everything that made his father famous: Scott felt he had no luck or talent or "the blue eyes." Scott was frustrated by his lack of achievement despite the promising roles he'd done because he did not feel he could compete with a father who was larger than life.

Scott was dealing with serious alcoholism by 1977, living by working odd labor jobs and sleeping on the floors of the friends who would allow it. Paul Newman had hired both a doctor and a psychologist for his son, and it seemed Scott was willing to accept the help. However, after a motorcycle accident in 1978, Scott began taking painkillers and valium, among other drugs.

In November 1978, Paul Newman, who was working on a theater production at the time, received notice that 28-year-old Scott had died from an overdose on drugs and alcohol in a motel room. Paul Newman confessed to Hotchner and others that he would always live with the guilt of his son's death.

Newman's grief, sadness and guilt over Scott's death compelled him to find a way to help others when he founded and established the Scott Newman Foundation with Joanne. The goal of the organization was to prevent drug abuse through education. The Scott Newman Foundation also sponsors the Rowdy Ridge Gang Camp, summer camps for families that are dealing with substance abuse issues.

Champion Race Car Driver

Though he came to racing late in his life (at about age 45) Newman steadily improved his racing skills through the 1970s and made many close friends along the way. Whenever he raced, he drew a great deal of attention, both from the crowds and the paparazzi. His friend Bob Sharp (of Bob Sharp Datsun) felt that Paul was able to ignore this almost overwhelming attention and just focus on driving, but the other drivers were eager to beat him. There was an attitude that Newman was not a serious driver, "just an actor," goofing around because he had the money and that he'd already been lucky enough. Surely he didn't need to win races, too.

But Newman loved the camaraderie of the other drivers. He also met, and he and Joanne both became good friends with Jim "Fitzy" Fitzgerald, who drove for the same team. Fitzy was close to Paul's age, and they were both much older than most of the other drivers. A lot of good-natured ribbing went on, with younger drivers offering to help the older men pay for their dentures - just for example. Fitzy and Newman competed against each other dozens of times, but there were never any hard feelings when one beat the other. They remained consistently helpful and supportive of one another.

In 1975, Newman formed the PLN Racing Team (PLN being his initials, remember), and Newman competed in many races all over the country, with his enthusiasm for the sport prompting him to schedule his acting career around his racing career, rather than the other way around.

Through racing, Newman also met a young black driver, Willy T. Ribbs, who was experiencing difficulties in obtaining spots on racing teams, outside of simply working for the pit crew. Ribbs was a well-known and controversial figure for his outspoken personality and for having a bit of a temper. Newman was instrumental in recommending Ribbs as a driver for the Trans Am racing team - for whom Ribbs went on to win 17 races. Years later, Ribbs became the first black driver to tour the circuit and race in the Indianapolis 500. In the documentary *Winning: The Racing Life of Paul Newman,* Ribbs credits Newman graciously and wholeheartedly and feels that if it had not been for Newman's speaking up on his behalf, he would never have gotten the opportunities that he eventually did.

After the death of Scott Newman in 1978, a strange new seriousness overtook Newman on the racetrack. Though his friends asked him if he would rather stop racing and deal with his grief, he instead asked to be allowed to race as much as possible. It was a relief to him, as it drove all other thoughts out of his mind. Scott's death also gave Newman a new inner fortitude; he was no longer "psyched out" by other drivers or cars; his focus was entirely on his own car and the road. In the year of Scott's death, Newman won 15 out of 17 races. He participated in the 24 hours of Daytona and then asked Dick Barbour, a highly respected driver, to team up with him for the 24 hours race at Le Mans in 1979.

Le Mans is widely considered the "elite" racing championship; all drivers want a chance to compete in the famous race. It includes both a raceway and a section of regular highway in France during both daylight and nighttime hours, regardless of weather conditions and requires highly skilled driving. Each team consists of three drivers. Newman and Dick Barbour raced with Rolf Stommelen. Their car was a Porsche 935.

The press coverage of Newman's participation was intense. European press acted extremely aggressive about getting close to Newman for an interview, going so far as to climb the walls of the house in which the team was staying and climbing into the pit stop on the raceway. The team did its best to keep the press off Newman. The conditions at Le Mans were brutal that year, including a night of rain and fog, with road conditions so bad that only 22 of the 55 cars entered actually managed to finish the race. Though they were in first place until the final laps, car trouble forced the Barbour team to take an extra-long pit stop and then take extra precautions on the final lap. They ended up finishing the race in second place, and they took first place in their class. This excellent performance solidified Newman's reputation as a first-class driver.

No longer was he considered an "actor with a hobby."

Newman's Own

The Newman's Own line of food products began in 1982. The common story is that Newman complained about disliking the salad dressing at a restaurant and decided to create his own, with his friend, writer A.E. Hotchner, a neighbor of Newman's, and a fellow philanthropist. At first, they gave the salad dressing as a gift to friends, but the reception was so positive that the two men decided to commercialize the product. Newman had toyed with the idea of opening a restaurant under the name "Newman's Own," but since that idea never really went anywhere, it was instead used as their new company's name.

When the label was designed to include Newman's face, he immediately knew that all the proceeds would have to go to charity - he was not comfortable with banking on his celebrity status for any other reason.

The line began with salad dressings but quickly expanded to include, among other products, popcorn (a personal favorite snack of his, as we know!), pasta sauce, salsa, wine, and lemonade, and even dog food and dog treats. After taxes, all proceeds from the line were donated to charity. As the years went by, the brand became a juggernaut of charitable donations.

Newman in the 1980s

I n 1977, Newman worked once again with George Roy Hill on the hockey film *Slap Shot* (a movie which has gained a cult following since then in the sports-movie arena for its irreverent look at old-school hockey). This comedy, however, was the end of an era for Newman, and the next decade took him on a new path. Newman was over 50 years old now and moving on to more mature parts.

In the 1980s, Newman selected certain roles to reinvent himself as an actor once more, turning in a series of performances that are considered some of his best. He began playing older, more embittered and troubled characters, yet men who were still up against "the system" and fighting lonely battles. He appeared in both *Fort Apache the Bronx* and *Absence of Malice* in 1981. In the first, he plays a cop who was trying to stay honest in the tough, impoverished precinct of the South Bronx. In the second, he is a businessman wrongly implicated by the FBI and the press in a mob murder who goes after justice for himself.

However, Newman seemed to hit his perfect note in the film *The Verdict* (1982), widely regarded as his greatest performance. *Premiere Magazine* actually ranks it at #19 in a list of the 100 all-time greatest performances (in case you were wondering, Fast Eddie Felson from *The Hustler* comes in at number 64). In *The Verdict,* Newman portrayed Frank Galvin, an alcoholic attorney who has had a number of career setbacks and eventually settled basically for being an ambulance chaser without much in the way of scruples. This is until he stumbles upon an "unwinnable" medical malpractice case for the family of a brain-damaged woman in a coma. The handling of the case has serious implications for Galvin's career: if he settles out of court, the case will win him thousands of dollars and a new start. However, he discovers the depth of the hospital's cover-up, and the corruption makes him angry enough that he decides to take the case to trial.

Newman says that he recognized all of Frank Galvin's frailties and that he connected deeply with the character. Watching the film, it is quite possible to forget that one is watching Newman at all, he disappears so far into the character that he almost ceases to look like himself. Newman was nominated for the Best Actor Oscar but lost that year to Ben Kingsley as Mahatma Gandhi.

Now, speaking of the Oscars: Newman's Oscar nominations for Best Actor up to that time were:

- ⌃ 1959, for Cat on a Hot Tin Roof
- ⌃ 1962, for The Hustler
- ⌃ 1964, for Hud
- ⌃ 1968, for Cool Hand Luke
- ⌃ 1982, for Absence of Malice
- ⌃ 1983, for The Verdict

By 1986, the Academy of Motion Pictures Arts and Sciences was beginning to feel rather guilty about Newman's unusual number of nominations without a win, considering his many contributions to the acting field. In 1986, therefore, he was given an Academy Honorary Award in recognition of his memorable performances, personal integrity, and his dedication to the craft. While this honorary award is certainly deserved, amusingly it was given to Newman when he still had three more acting Oscar nominations - and one win - to go.

The Return
of Fast Eddie Felson

The great American director Martin Scorsese was in charge of the sequel to *The Hustler,* which brought Paul Newman back to reprise his role as "Fast Eddie" Felson in the film *The Color of Money* (1986). Now 20 years older and a little wiser, Fast Eddie is out of the hustling business and making an honest living until he sees his way into a new hustle when he takes on the mentorship of a cocky but uncontrollable pool player (a young Tom Cruise, who was busily making a name for himself as a hot new movie star in his own right).

Newman recalls getting a painful lesson from Scorsese, who after several unsuccessful takes early in filming told Newman to stop trying to be funny - in a scene that was meant to be comical. Newman said he did as instructed, "after taking the knife out of his back." Following Scorsese's advice, even though it hurt, Newman played the movie absolutely straight, and his performance garnered him another Academy Award nomination.

However, as we saw, Newman had been so frequently nominated for the Best Actor Oscar that in 1986 when he was nominated yet again, he decided not to go to the ceremony. After all, he had been all but guaranteed the Oscar the year before, only to be ousted by the far more "Oscar-friendly" film Gandhi and actor Ben Kingsley. Newman stayed home from the Oscars that year - and won. His award was accepted for him by his good friend, director Robert Wise, who had some difficulty getting presenter Bette Davis to stop talking long enough for Wise to say anything on Paul's behalf.

Here is an interesting note: Newman is only one of six actors to be nominated for playing the same role in two different films. He was nominated for "Fast Eddie" Felson in both *The Hustler* and *The Color of Money*.

Newman the Actor
and Newman the Director

Insofar as his own acting career, Newman didn't want to take "leading man" roles. He wanted to take challenges and found his own work least effective when he was playing himself. For example, he did not like his work as Lew Harper, a sort of Bond-like secret agent for the United Nations in the films *Harper* and *The Drowning Pool*, because playing Harper was too much like playing himself.

One thing Newman consistently required out of any acting contract was two weeks of rehearsal time. He says studios agreed to it because they thought they were getting something for nothing, but in actuality, he believes it saves a production company millions of dollars in the long run to put actors together for a time period where they can get to know their characters. He likes to rehearse movie parts the way he rehearses theater parts. His friend Robert Redford wasn't a fan of rehearsals, as he felt they reduced the spontaneity of a performance, but he went along with them to appease Newman.

Paul has never felt he was a "natural" actor but a cerebral one. To him, acting requires a great deal of thought and self-examination. He called his wife

Joanne an intuitive actor who could slip in and out of a role easily. He never found it so, and never thought he had a gift to perform. However, he wanted to perform badly enough that he would force it out of himself.

He believed that he needed to look into a character and figure out what their valid rhythms, mannerisms and thought processes were. He made these choices about characters and then found a way to make them organic. Newman says that his wife Joanne, on the other hand, goes for the organic part of a character first, and then rounds it out with rhythms and mannerisms.

This understanding of the different ways in which actors can approach roles, he believed, was the key to being a successful director. As he felt that "method acting" meant that every individual actor had his or her own method, as a director, he felt it was his duty to work differently with every actor. A director is meant to give actors confidence and liberate them so they dare to try things.

Newman directed six films from 1968 through 1987. Four of his six directed films starred his wife, including *Rachel, Rachel* (1968), for which she received an Oscar nomination; *The Effect of Gamma Rays on Man-in-the-Moon Marigolds* (1972), for which she received a Golden Globe; *The Shadow Box* (1980); and *The Glass Menagerie* (1987).

In 1971, Newman took over directing *Sometimes a Great Notion* (from a novel by Ken Kesey) when Richard A. Colla was fired. Newman was already starring in the film. He found the dual role of directing and starring to be difficult. This is entirely believable, as Newman was a highly focused worker who put all of his energies into a job, including intense preparation. Doing two jobs at once seems not only like not a great deal of pressure but quite the opposite of how he preferred to tackle a project. The film is best remembered now for having several great actors working together, including Henry Fonda.

Regardless of his trepidation to work as both actor and director, Newman did take on the dual role once again in 1984 when he directed and starred in *Harry and Son,* along with Robby Benson. The pair played a widowed father and his adult son who come to odds over the generation gap in their work ethics.

The Transformation
of Paul Newman's Racing Career

After the Barbour team's tremendous performance at Le Mans, most of Newman's family, friends, and fellow race car drivers anticipated that he would stop racing. He was almost 60 years old, and racing is generally considered a "young man's sport." More than that, though, those who cared for him began to worry about how hard he was pushing himself on the track. He began to take increasingly alarming risks and make errors on the track, some of which resulted in crashes.

There were still some enjoyable moments to be had on the track. While making *The Color of Money* in 1986, Newman got his co-star, young Tom Cruise, interested in racing as well. He introduced Cruise to his friends Mario Andretti, Bob Sharp and Bob Bondurant, and for a year or so, they trained and raced together. Bob Sharp recalls that Cruise was not interested in taking time to develop the skills for real racing; however, he did well enough to place in a couple of races, and he was also able to make the film *Days of Thunder* with the skills he had acquired by training with Bob Bondurant. But being involved in a race track crash convinced Cruise that professional racing was just not for him.

Tragically, Newman suffered the loss of two friends: first, his Le Mans teammate Rolf Stommelen was killed in a crash in the LA Grand Prix. Then in 1987, his old friend and racing partner Jim "Fitzy" Fitzgerald was killed when his car hit the barrier during a race in which Newman was also driving. Newman went two more laps and then quit, too distraught to drive any further.

After that, Newman became a team owner. His friend Mario Andretti convinced him to pair up with Carl Haas and form the Newman Haas Racing Team (which would also include Andretti's son, Michael, as a primary driver). Carl Haas was very unlike Newman; he was hyper, intense, and emotional, whereas Newman was always grounded, laid-back and friendly. At first, the two men did not seem to even get along (Newman would not have ever agreed to work with Haas, if not for Andretti's intervention), but over the years they developed a working relationship that became quite effective. Somehow, these two managed to work well together, each working off the other's strengths, to create a racing team that was extremely successful (winning 108 races and eight championships) and full of devoted members, who still speak of their time racing for and working with the Newman Haas team as their best years in the racing world.

The Hole
in the Wall Gang Camp

Perhaps the most famous and heartfelt of Newman's charities, The Hole in the Wall Gang Camp, based in Ashford, Connecticut, is a nonprofit organization for the benefit of seriously ill children and their families. Newman founded the camp in 1988 with the goal to give these children the opportunity to experience the friendship and spiritual healing of camp. The Hole in the Wall Gang Camp provides not only residential summer camps but year-round services to children with cancer and other life-threatening illnesses and an outreach program that can take the fun of summer camp to hospitals and other places where children are treated. In his own words, Newman says that he wanted to make a place where kids could just be kids and "raise a little hell," and he remembered with great affection his own childhood camping days doing just that.

Children from ages 7 to 15 are eligible, and the original camp has facilities enough for over 1000 children. Children with cancer, sickle cell anemia, hemophilia or other life-threatening illnesses whose lives are disrupted by courses of treatment and the stress and pain of illness are here given an opportunity to enjoy the normal summer activities of childhood while still seeing to their safety and any special needs.

In 1986, Newman and his friend A.E. Hotchner approached the renowned Dr. Howard Pearson, a pediatric hematologist/oncologist, about creating a camp for children who had cancer or other serious diseases. Dr. Pearson established the medical support necessary for such a camp to succeed and spent the first fourteen summers at the camp as the on-site physician. The camp's lake, Pearson Pond, is named after him.

The Hole in the Wall Gang Camp was built on a 300-acre parcel of land, that includes a 44-acre lake, which Newman bought from his neighbors, the Harkalays after they refused other offers to let the land be developed for commercial purposes. Newman named the camp after the gang in the movie *Butch Cassidy and the Sundance Kid.* The camp has a child-sized reproduction of a western town but also a state-of-the-art medical hospital. Newman spent many days there himself, often fishing with the campers on Pearson Pond.

The Hole in the Wall Gang Camp provides year-long outreach programs to about 20,000 seriously ill children, their families, and the hospitals that serve them, all free of charge, with the understanding of the enormous stress an illness can place on all the members of a family. The summer camps include week-long sessions for children diagnosed with a serious or life-threatening illness, a session for their healthy siblings, and sessions for the entire family during which they can relax and reconnect with each other in a natural environment. The activities are all those normally associated with camp and the great outdoors: fishing, swimming, archery, sports, horseback riding and crafts (and some really adventurous-looking activities too - ballooning and zip-lining!); but these are all offered in an environment that is safe for the children, which takes into account their differing needs and has medical facilities on-site to deal with any urgent care needs. Newman made it a point that every child at the camp can participate in every activity.

Team Hole in the Wall is the Camp's fundraising group. For this initiative, amateur athletes raise money by participating in athletics events, such as cycling events and marathons, including the Boston Marathon and the New York City Marathon. Participation in Team Hole in the Wall events increases every year.

The camp is funded not only by Team Hole in the Wall and the Newman's Own Foundation but by contributions from other organizations and 25,000 annual donors, including Paul Newman's college fraternity, Phi Kappa Tau. The camp is a member of the SeriousFun Children's Network, which is an association of camps situated around the world for seriously ill children.

A.E. Hotchner (who was affectionately known as "Hotch" throughout the camp) continued to be a part of the camp's activities, building the camp theater and writing sketches for annual fundraisers or just being a part of activities at the campgrounds. Hotchner died in February of 2020 at the age of 102, and the camp's website memorialized him with great affection, showing several pictures of Hotch and Newman goofing off at the camp with their smiling guests.

Newman's Films
in the 1990s and Beyond

At a time when many actors of Newman's age might be slowing down or limiting their film appearances to cameos, Newman simply looked upon "retirement age" as another chance to challenge himself. In 1989 and 1990 when he was turning 65, he released three films in which he had starring roles: *Fat Man and Little Boy; Blaze;* and *Mr. & Mrs. Bridge* (with wife Joanne).

In 1994, Newman had a villainous role in the cult-favorite film *The Hudsucker Proxy* but really won everybody's heart as the lovable loser Sully in *Nobody's Fool.* In this crowd-pleasing film, he is an irresponsible old rascal who is forced to confront some realities when his estranged son moves back to town. Newman's portrayal of Sully won him yet another Oscar nomination, his eighth.

In 1998, Newman took an interesting role as the personal assistant to a rich couple under the threat of blackmail in a neo-noir thriller called *Twilight,* alongside Susan Sarandon and Gene Hackman. The film benefitted from the still-got-it sex appeal of both Newman (who was well over 70 years old) and

Sarandon (over 50), an anti-hero and a femme fatale made to trouble each other.

In what was really Newman's final big-screen role (other than voice acting), he took another unusual turn as a ruthless Irish gangster in the film *Road to Perdition* (2003), working alongside Tom Hanks. Newman, who plumbed the depths of a terrifyingly analytical gangster willing to sacrifice those he loves, got his ninth Oscar nomination for this film; this time for best Supporting Actor. He was almost 80 years old at the time.

After *Road to Perdition,* Newman narrated some other documentaries and appeared on a couple of television productions. His final starring film role, however, had a somewhat different flavor and was a tribute to the man's love of racing and, well, cars.

Cars (2006)

Newman's final major film appearance was as a voice actor for the Pixar film, *Cars*. Newman provided the voice of Doc Hudson, a retired Hudson Hornet (stock cars which raced during the 1950s). Director John Lasseter credits Newman with tremendous knowledge of racing and cars and used Newman's insights to build on the character of Doc Hudson and ensure that all the driving advice Doc Hudson was giving to hotshot car Lightning McQueen was absolutely correct.

In fact, Newman was fully aware of the racing history of Hudson Hornets and was only too glad to fill Lasseter in on all the details. In the recording booth, Lasseter and Newman had long conversations about racing, and they recorded everything Newman said. (It was in this way that Doc Hudson was able to make a flashback appearance in *Cars 3* (2017), many years after Paul Newman's death.)

The film *Cars* is listed in *Autotrader's* "Top 6 Movies about Cars" alongside *The Fast and the Furious, Bullitt, Gone in 60 Seconds, Baby Driver,* and *Max Mad: Fury Road.*

Newman's Own
Foundation's Continuing Work

Along with writer Hotchner, Newman co-authored the book *Shameless Exploitation in Pursuit of the Common Good* in 2003, in which they playfully detailed their triumphant turn to marketing in order to raise money for charity. There was a time, you will recall, when Newman didn't believe he could find any passion in merchandising.

The charitable proceeds of the Newman's Own Foundation go to many different causes, including:

1. An annual award called the First Amendment Award, for protection of the First Amendment as it applies to writing;

2. $250,000 in Catholic Relief services to aid Kosovo refugees;

3. Ongoing major donations to The Mirror Theater, Ltd., a theater company designed to help actors learn their craft by putting them in a variety of roles in a single season. This is traditional "alternating repertory," which is a classic theater style and has produced and been associated with an incredible variety of respected actors;

4. A grant to the MINDS Foundation to fund its nonprofit work in India;

5. The New York Times Neediest Cases Fund, which has since 1912 distributed charitable donations to the needy in New York City, evolving from selecting specific cases to highlight to an organization that contributes to seven participating social welfare agencies;

6. Shining Hope for Communities, an organization that promotes better lives for girls and woman in the Kibera slum of Nairobi, Kenya;

7. The Safe Water Network, which works in local sustainability of water systems in areas such as India and Ghana;

8. Edible Schoolyard: This program runs in Berkeley California, at Martin Luther King Jr. Middle School, where students are involved in the planting, harvesting and preparation of crops;

9. The Fisher House Foundation, which builds homes where military families can stay free of charge while a family member is in the hospital; they are built close to the hospitals they serve;

10. Pilgrim's Hospices, a charitable hospice organization in Great Britain; and

11. The WILD Young Women Programme of New Zealand. WILD stands for Wisdom, Integrity, Love for Yourself, Discover Who You Are. This program is open for girls from ages 12 to 17 who are having difficulties in coping with dysfunctional situations and/or families. The goal is to help them learn skills to cope with social relationships, sexual behaviors and self-destructive behaviors.

In the year of Newman's death, 2008, Newman's Own Foundation donated over $20 million to a variety of charities. Its charitable work has continued in earnest since that time and has donated over $500 million total to charity since its formation in 1982.

Charity Beyond
Newman's Own Foundation

Of course, it should also be noted that some of Newman's philanthropic endeavors have come from outside of the Newman's Own Foundation.

Paul and Joanne donated $10 million to Kenyon College to establish a scholarship fund.

Newman was also integral in participating in the maintenance of Aspetuck Land Trust, a nonprofit conservation organization in Connecticut. His estate gifted a large portion of his personal property to the town of Westport, Connecticut. The Land Trust continues to operate by promoting ways of combating climate change on a local level and reconnecting the forests of Connecticut that have been disrupted by construction. The Newman Poses Preserve (which is Newman's donated property along with that donated by his neighbor, Lillian Poses) is the only public memorial approved by Newman's family to honor their late father.

In 2006, Newman opened a restaurant which he named "The Dressing Room," the profits of which went toward the Westport Country

Playhouse. Newman worked with the Westport Country Playhouse on numerous occasions as a director and performer.

Newman was also a co-founder of the Committee Encouraging Corporate Philanthropy (CECP) in 1999. The coalition has since changed its name to Chief Executives for Corporate Purpose. Over 200 of the world's largest companies are involved in the coalition. Its various initiatives are too many to list here, but their overall mission statement is to "create a better world through business," by giving to charity and investing in society and the companies' own employees.

Philanthropic Awards

K ennedy Center Honors are annual awards given to members of the performing arts community who have contributed significantly to American culture. Paul Newman and Joanne Woodward were one of only three married couples to receive the rainbow-striped awards together in 1992. At the ceremony, children from the Hole in the Wall Gang Camp were introduced by Robert Redford and appeared on stage to thank the couple themselves, causing both Newman and Woodward to wipe tears from their eyes as they were given a standing ovation.

The Academy of Motion Picture Arts and Sciences has its own award for contributions to humanitarian causes, called the Jean Hersholt Humanitarian Award. Newman received the award in 1994.

Also in 1994, Newman and Woodward were awarded the Jefferson Award, sponsored by the American Institute for Public Service, for "Outstanding Public Servicing Benefiting the Disadvantaged."

Newman was adamant in his conviction that taking his own rewards and spreading them around was a far greater reward than acting or anything else for that matter. He said that if he could share a little of the luck he was given, he was obligated to do so and that if he was somehow afforded the luxury of being a public figure, he should use that power to benefit others.

Newman's daughters have participated in his conservations and philanthropic efforts. Elinor, after appearing in two of the films her father directed, turned to conservation work and founded the organics section of the "Newman's Own" products line. Melissa Newman teaches acting classes to prison inmates. Claire Newman took over the SeriousFun organization (which runs the Hole in the Wall Gang Camp and its outreach programs).

One Last Lap

N ewman's last appearance on Broadway was in 2002 when he played the Stage Manager in an *Our Town* revival which had a successful run, despite lukewarm critical reviews. He had planned to direct *Of Mice and Men* at the Westport Country Playhouse in Connecticut but withdrew because of health reasons a few months before rehearsals were to begin.

Newman withdrew from acting when he knew he was no longer capable of working at the level he would want to. He spent his last couple years of life mostly out of the public eye.

At the age of 82, Paul Newman, driving a Trans Am, raced and won at Lime Rock Raceway in Connecticut.

The following year, he visited the track after a lengthy absence. Many of his friends there, like Mario Andretti, felt a certainty that he had come to the track to say goodbye. He had not allowed anyone to know about or become involved in his illness, but it was clear that he was weak. Unable to drive himself, Newman sat in the back of a station wagon and allowed himself to be driven around the Lime Rock race track. It was truly a place he considered home to many wonderful memories and a place of special importance in his heart.

Paul Newman was a longtime smoker and died from lung cancer on September 26, 2008, at the age of 83, in Westport, Connecticut. Few people were aware of the extent of his illness; even Hotch, his longtime pal, knew of the diagnosis but not the struggle that Newman was having with it. As was always the case, Paul Newman lived his private life privately, without any desire for undue attention.

In the year before his death, Joanne and Paul celebrated their 50-year wedding anniversary. Joanne says the secret of their long marriage was that he kept her laughing. Their relationship was built on a strong foundation because they had been good friends before they became lovers. They trusted each other and could tell each other anything. Of his wife, Paul said that there was no one who supported him more. Even during his racing career, which she considered a dangerous hobby, she was unconditionally supportive.

After Newman's death, Joanne Woodward withdrew for the most part from celebrity life, and the roles she has taken since then have been limited to voice acting.

Paul was survived by his brother Arthur Newman Jr., who said that he, Arthur, was actually the luckier of the two men, "because he got to have Paul Newman as a brother."

Newman's daughters have in various capacities taken over his charitable work.

Conclusion

When Paul Newman died, the world reacted and grieved as if it had lost a friend. This is understandable, as he was a popular public figure for over six decades with one of the most well-known faces in the world. The New York Times credited him with taking the sullen "rebel" American male of the 60s and making him a "likable renegade." Not only was he talented and beloved as an actor and respected as a championship driver, he was a renowned "good guy" who gave back an incredible amount to the world that afforded him such luck.

Obituaries called him one of the "last great 20th century actors." Truly, he had never rested on his laurels but kept reinventing his craft during each decade of his life. It was never a sure thing, what Paul Newman would do next, but the chances were good that he would do it in the best way possible with all seriousness of effort but without ever losing his enthusiasm for fun and friendship. Alongside that hard-working, intense ethic for his craft, though, his friends and family remember him as a man of great humor and great passion for life. His passion showed in everything he did.

In reviewing Newman's long life and multiple careers, it is easy to see both sides of the man: the careful, serious workman and the affectionate, funny best friend. As with any life, he had his share of troubles and tragedies.

Yet overall, and probably thanks to his own attitude of determination to do his best at everything he tried, his grounded faith in family, ethics and generosity and his own unfailing sense of life as an adventure, Newman never let himself be stopped by tragedy. He always seemed to find a way to turn misfortune into an opportunity to make the world a better place. Mixed with a streak of luck that feels a lot like karma, Newman lived a charmed life and left an amazing legacy.

Printed in Great Britain
by Amazon

80982376R00048